CW00687174

The Runaway Stars

The Runaway Stars

A Collection of Poems

L NATALE

Copyright © 2023, 2024 L Natale

All rights reserved. No part of this book may be reproduced or used in any manner without the prior written permission of the copyright owner, except for the use of brief quotations in a book review.

This is for you, just the way you are.

INTRODUCTION

As a kid, I remember watching the movie, *Peggy Sue Got Married*, and the part I liked best was the scene with the beat poet/ motorcycle rider, Michael Fitzsimmons. Michael and Peggy spent a night together under the stars, as he recited a poem to her by William Butler Yeats. Later, when she woke up from her coma/trip back in 1986 again, she had a copy of his poetry book on the hospital nightstand, dedicated to "Peggy Sue, and a Starry Night." Well, that looked pretty good to me, even at 7 years old - though I had no idea what was *actually* going on between them under the starry night sky...

When my teen years came, poetry turned into something necessary for survival (hyperbole is appropriate when discussing teenage stuff). I joined the poetry club at school - *Scribes*. What a terrible name. There were plenty of black turtlenecks in the group, but nobody was as cool as Michael Fitzsimmons. That was a bit disappointing.

When I was 17, I came into possession of a book that changed everything about what poetry *could be*. I'd found Carl Sandburg, and his book *Complete Poems*. You might have read one of Sandburg's most famous poems in high school too - a short one called *Fog*, about said fog coming in on little cat feet. It was used a lot to teach metaphor. That's probably how I knew about him in the first place.

My copy of his masterwork was a navy linen-covered edition published in 1950 that belonged to Nadine C. Hill, who wrote her name on the front page. When the book came into my hands (I can't remember how I ended up with it - it kind of just appeared like Sauron's Ring, but with much better results for me than Frodo and the LOTR gang), I signed my name in the book just below Nadine's. It became my very own 'precious,' and I proceeded to write all sorts of notations, underlines, and even some silly swirly things (why, teenage me?), to mark my preferred passages. I loved that freaking book - took it everywhere.

His work is in the public domain now, so I can share one of my many favorites with you here:

Two by Carl Sandburg
Memory of you is...a blue spear of flower.
I cannot remember the name of it.
Alongside a bold dripping poppy is fire and silk.
                    And they cover you.

My poetry was never the same after this. I was influenced by Sandburg's broad perspective, stunning visual imagery, and ability to apply his keen reporter skills to prose and verse. I fell into step with his experience of the World Wars and felt a kinship to the 'Hog Butcher' of the world - Chicago.

He wrote beautiful vignettes of real people too. A few unforgettable lines from the poem *Mag*, in the *Chicago Poems* published first in 1916:

I wish to God I never saw you, Mag.
I wish to God the kids had never come.

Sandburg collected authentic moments and captured them. This was not just another pile of romantic B.S. More than anything, this kind of poetry made me *feel* something.

In my freshman year of college, I took a required course called Life Planning, or some such nonsense, and the major assignment was to make a 'life map.' This was kind of like a vision board but layered onto an idealized timeline. The professor asked us to create a vision of a *perfect life* - what would a career look like family, goals, travels, hobbies, etc., all the way up to an imaginary end of the line of projected death.

I thought it was a silly assignment back then, but honestly, it's uncanny how many things on that poster paper came to pass, and pretty darn close to how I drew it out. The most outrageous wish for my imaginary future was one that had not yet manifested from the poster plan.

My dream 'hobby' was to be a writer of poetry books - well to be precise, a *Pulitzer Prize-winning* poetry writer. The Professor said to dream big, and I'm good at following directions. In my perfectly crafted life, I would win the *Pulitzer Prize* for my third poetry collection, so I left some room in there for humility…ha!

I chose my major later that year - a degree in Literature and Writing, and throughout my studies at University, I never found anyone's poetry I loved more than Sandburg's.

So, I kept on writing throughout my schooling, and at one point I remember reading back a poem and thinking, hey, that's actually kind of *good*. It didn't seem like I'd even written it. That was the start of access to the flow state where, like the Romantic Era Poets I was studying, I was able to *negate* myself. Out flowed the words from somewhere beyond whatever *I* was.

In the winter of my twentieth year, I stared out a window at the Spanish Steps in Rome from the final apartment of my favorite Romantic Era poet, John Keats. In that very room, Keats, took his last stab at staying alive, as he was in a pretty serious battle with tuberculosis. Unfortunately, he died young - only twenty-five years old. I was young like him too and felt deeply connected to the spirit of Keats as I stared at his death mask. In his short life, he chose poetry over being a doctor. He chose to make eternally cherished word creations over the stability of the pharmacy. *I was in awe.*

So yes, I was neck-deep into the whole poetry dream at that point. Then, life happened.

After I graduated with my Lit/Writing degree, I realized the best chance of making money with that major was to become a teacher. Next, I got married to a wonderful man, and we had kids of our own.

Unlike Keats, who chose the poetry road, I took the practical road.

Poetry dried up. *The Complete Poems* of Carl Sandburg gathered dust on the shelf. My dream of writing *Pulitzer Prize-worthy* poems faded like the marker on that old poster. The stars were officially out of my eyes.

Then, get this…the stars brought it all back to me full circle when in an odd deviation of the poster plan, I became a practicing astrologer. Over the years, I've had the privilege to read a lot of people's charts. All kinds of beautiful people, all kinds of stories, all the archetypes playing in different variations. Each one of them is a poem.

One such reading was with a poet who wanted to pursue professional poetry at a higher level. My first reaction was, "Can people publish poetry books for a living?" I had gone so far into my practical mode (does that seem like an oxymoron coming from an astrologer?) that I was quite curious because honestly, I still wanted to be a poet deep down under all that dust. Could he do it? And if he could, could I do it too? Yes to both. Why not?

When I read his collection of work, a new world of possibilities for my writing opened back up - the walls holding back a reservoir of words started to crack. Carl Sandburg came off the shelf and reclaimed a spot on the bedside table. I started to write again, and wow, it felt *good*.

With this first collection of poems, *The Runaway Stars*, I'm fulfilling my end-of-the-poster board bargain from 1996. Now that I think about it, I kind of remember making myself pretty 'old' (to a 17-year-old, anyways, which was around 40-ish) when I got the poetry books going, so maybe I'm on track after all. Whether or not the Pulitzer Prize committee ever picks up on my work, well that's to be determined. In any case, I'll give them until book three before I start bugging them…

I hope my jump off the high dive to fulfilling my dream inspires you to take a risk and follow your passion as well. Self-expression is one of the keys to authentic happiness - I want to be happy, how about you? Enough holding ourselves back, because reality is *malleable*, not set in stone. Just make a poster and see for yourself.

The Runaway Stars are poems painted in shades of reality and gathered through the lens of fantasy. They travel through tales of past lives and trek through dreams of future ones. The throughline of this collection is the experience of impermanence and resolution. All that being said, I humbly invite you to join me on a journey through the land of runaway stars.

L Natale
Valley Center, California
July 2023

Enter the realm of

The Runaway Stars

THE RUNAWAY STARS

I found you amongst the runaway stars -
you were their equal,
as wild and as free

like all vast things,
you said I was fine,
that I could just *be*

Tell me the ancient truth only you know -
show me the sky
with no eyes to see

like a nightjar,
I have your star space
to explore, and sing

When you lived amongst runaway stars,
you heard them whisper,
saw them weaving
a beautiful tapestry
of cosmic breathing

Hold me close in your silky black night -
tell me again what they said to you
about living,
and
never dying at all-
ever at all.

LIFT OF THE SEA

We had a boat with a tricky sail -
and water with no end
Most of what remains of our time
is a faint, sun-faded memory

What do you recall?
The storms with clouds that would
twist and spin?
The lift of the sea beneath us?
The tilt of the hull?

We moved by the stars in the sky,
we lived by the ever-changing moon,
we were reckless in everything -
chasing dreams,
leaving wounds

The longest shadows follow me still:

a tune you picked up on the island
and never stopped playing

the fine layer of
sea salt crystals glittering
on the port side window

the sun on my face,
your hands letting go of my waist,
and the glare of the sea,
when I told you we two
would soon become three

INTO THE NIGHT

she will take you with her
listen to all your stories

she will let you have her,
be your highest high

she will know everything you want
fulfill your great desires

she will give all of herself freely

until she is
empty
and lost

filled
with all of
you

left
with none of
her

in all this giving,
she will be of no use

she will lose once more,
when you turn away
and disappear into the night

LIVE INSIDE MY BONES

When the words are gone,
and the phantom fires fade
I crave your guidance -
I need you

Come to me, Daimon,*
bring me everything but flowers...
I want dead languages
and mysteries to solve -
I want you

You are a respite
from this lonesome mind
so please let me repay your kindness
with things more treasured than gold

Come to me Diamon,
hear this tortured call
come live inside my bones
I'm ready for it all

* "If we must reveal to you the truth concerning one's personal Daimon we must say that he is not distributed to us from one part of the heavens nor from any of the visible planets but from the entire cosmos - its multi-faceted life and its multi-form body - through which the soul descends into generation. And when the soul selects them as their leader the Daimon immediately attends to the task of fulfilling the lives of the soul to the body when it descends." ~Iamblichus c.245 – c. 325

DESERT TAKE ME

Cicadas sing their one-tone song,
heat overwhelms my senses
I look at you with your open shirt and golden skin -
you are a memory in the making
Dark glasses reflect the chlorine cobalt waters
that don't belong in this midcentury memory
Your smile is the only oasis
I would walk blurry miles to cool myself in

Desert, take me if this is the kind of heat you can bring

NO INK

I change too much
don't like to commit
any tattoo I would ever get
would be irrelevant
no matter how much it meant
in the moment

The only thing that would remain
a permanent stain of memory -
someone I once was, but have grown out of

And I would groan at seeing
my worn-out reflection -
some different person of the past
living in the same marked flesh

There would be an even bigger
disconnect to the body I'm in
a marker permanent upon my skin
is too much attachment to impermanence

Nostalgia is melancholy -
it hurts more than it pleases,
and memory lane is a place that changes
every time you walk down her street

ON THE OLD TRAIL

Where should we go now, my dear?
We are simple hobos searching
for something more than home-

Shall we hide in the boxcars,
or jump off the track?
We can go anywhere,
except going back,
'cause we're memorable and wanted
in all the worst ways

We'll stay loyal until we can't
'till they beat us
and push our faces into the floor...
even the strongest can break
'cause we're hated and chased
in all the worst ways

Despite all that they've done,
no matter what they'll do,
I'll keep a secret compartment
for the lonesome trail,
for freedom,
for you -
for the things we've never tried
for the places, we've never seen,
for all of this, my dear,
I'll keep a part of my coal smoke heart
extra clean

JUST A TASTE

I believe what I've heard
in the choirs
of sacred spaces,
chanting for God

I believe what I've seen
in the mirrors
of telescope faces,
searching for God

I believe what I've read
in the words
of a poem's fine laces
reaching for God

All play their fractal part
to illuminate
what little can be faced
of the infinite reality of God

through communion
through patterns
through voices in unison -

all pass for grace,
but you and I know
it's only just a taste

FOREVER

There is a deep longing
for the belonging of love
without judgment
without fear
so hear me now

I love you

I love your deep river flowing -
it also runs through me
we are one person growing -
merge in eternal seas

Here we become love,
we embody it
swim in it
breathe in it
give it with open hearts
with open hands

In this calm water
we show what we are
a mosaic of pure radiant love

You must know by now
how precious and adored you are?

Listen to the truth in this whisper,
put the seashell to your ear -
I love you…

Yes, can you hear it?

I love you, and that is all
you'll ever need to know

BELONG TO YOU

split into four,
or a thousand,
or infinity,
and live all those lives
simultaneously -
I will always want more

one is music
one is words
one is adventure
one is sin

you are a book I never want to end

YOUR BRIGHTNESS IS THE SUN

You've let me in to see you
our time was never done
I'm watching very closely
your brightness is the sun

Your brightness is the sun
through a clear prism glass
All the colors scatter
they move to let you pass

They move to let you pass
as I stay by your side
I like everything about you
there's nothing left to hide

There's nothing left to hide
no depth I can not bear
for depth lives in me too
it's absolutely everywhere

It's absolutely everywhere
that I would gladly follow
we'll walk the fine raised scar lines
we'll purge until we're hollow

BLANKET OF THE NIGHT

Covered and caressed, fully complete
in the blanket of the night

Nothing more is needed, all is released
in the blanket of the night

Can you see how it looks,
can you feel how it feels,
when we meet under these stars?

I'll cover you with this sky -
with the black velvet swirls,
and we will go deep
into the pink nebula nurseries
to witness their births,
a next generation
of pure power and energy

Sitting with you
under the blanket of the night
we can see everything so clearly
in the dark

UNDER IT ALL

What is beneath all of this blood and skin?

Last week, I was done being flesh and bone, overwhelmed with
the fatigue of being 'myself,' because I know the truth -

I am not me

In the sparkling waves of darkness, I saw that *"I am"* is not real
in any important way

I'm a vehicle, the latest model of borrowed elements
from the earth, for whatever remains constant
from body to body

I'm a series of choices over time,
another unique journey to add to the never-ending pile

GO HUNGRY

What is it like to feel filled,
not hungry?
I'm always hungry for more,
wanting to see behind
a thousand doors -
to understand what it all means
and how it feels to be clean
from all this desire

I want
not wanting
anything

But, there is always something to chase,
a silly white rabbit to follow
a hunger to fill
a drive to take

I can't shake it
I can't let go of the hunger
this life I'm living
dissolves over and again
to wanting more

SHUT UP FOREVER

too many words,
never without the hum of thought -
shut up forever

an angry old toad woman
loves the sound
of her own
lips flapping

incessant
words
never stop

looping
thoughts
never stop

a voice inside,
argues with itself
to the point
where the only logical
thing that can be said

is

kindly
shut up forever
amen

NO PLACE ELSE TO GO

There is a confession
upon the lips
upon the tip
of the tongue

Words are trickling
and dripping
into the recesses
of the mind

What is desired
would be very bad
to have
in these hands

The confession creeps
into sleeping dreams
crawling back
from the brink

It finds shadows
to curl into
and still waters
in which to sink

Be quiet, confession -
you are chaos
between
clenched teeth

IN YOUR PLACE

Sometimes I imagine
what it would be like
to be in your place

What are your demons
saying to you?

I can think
of at least
one thing…

ROYALS

The crow and the coyote
what a pair of disregarded rulers
on the fringe of everything
cleaning up the mess

These underworld royals
feast on the dead
and face the living
eye to eye

Crow King,
Coyote Queen,
She can run,
He can fly

Recognize
that they rule all,
because everything
eventually dies

COLD STILL PLACE

In the cold, still place I will wait.
You have been here before, and know it well.
We are passing ships on the plane of stars,
navigating home in the dark, alone.
Reach out your hand to point back in my direction,
I'll be here - I'm your reflection.
Like a hole in the cosmic lace,
like the memory of your face,
we begin and end in this cold, still place.

HOOKED

Hooked in, like a fish,
so easily baited
fully knowing on the other end
of that tasty bite is certain death,
not just danger.

Still, it is a good way to go,
satisfied, with a belly full.

So make it a silver hook,
to match your silver tongue.

Make me a tasty dish,
this fight's already won.

SKIES KEEP PRAYERS

Once there was a man who loved a woman - well, he thought he loved her, but did he? He prayed to the skies to make it so. He loved the idea of her, yes. He loved the idea of himself as he wanted to be. But was it she that he loved? Skies, keeper of his prayers, make it so.

Once there was a woman who wanted to be loved - well, she thought it was a love she wanted, but did she? She prayed to the skies to make it so. She loved the shape of her belly getting round. She loved the idea of herself in a family. But was it he that she loved? Skies, keeper of her prayers, make it so.

Once there was a child who never knew their love, or their prayers.

ANOTHER DOOR

If I could remove this layer of constriction, the structure of my restriction, the thing that keeps it all together, would I tell the truth and regret it? Yes. Right away I would without hesitation.

Borders and boundaries keep it all contained, and in those designated places, I can intertwine, I can aim toward the destination - a place beyond my human mind.

But then, there comes a time when the boundaries that keep me safely in feel like layers of suffocation - like claustrophobic contradictions, and I would kill for a can of lighter fluid, do anything for a match, so I could burn open another door and make an escape hatch.

RISE AGAIN

Is it possible to launch a love
built from a wreck of wounded words?

What is there to love,
other than the flotsam of confused meanings,
tangled in one's own ragged ropes?

We piece together
the broken bloody planks of this disaster
adrift on a sea of never-ending mystery
to make a useless raft.

The sea hides things in its depths -
other lost ships like ours
sunk to the bottom,
where it is too dark to let in real love,
and too deep for anything to rise again.

TIGER

She rattles the cage and stalks at the bars
Tiger, Tiger burning in her chains,
just below the surface, escape is close

Tiger, I feel you agitated, awake, ready to claw and maim
You can destroy with a swoop of your razor-capped claw -
just one quick move of your jaw will end most irritating things

You are made of black, orange, and white -
colors that let you own the shadows,
stalk your prey invisible, I know well your desires

Calm yourself now Tiger -
I am here to help
I will stop them from feeding you bad blood,
and one day soon, you shall be free

FROZEN FACES

I want to drink too much tonight.
I want to be bloodless.
I want no name,
no shame,
no games.

I want to break into fractals of light,
misty glitter shards,
and look the way stars appear
from this far distant Earth shore.

I want to know the truth.
I want to never really know anything.
I want to inhabit another form,
and hold the freedom of being
no one and nothing
in the palm of my hand.

Why do I keep coming around here
where I don't belong?
I'm drawn like a magnet, swirling around,
like the green lights of the north.

I want something that lives in the sky
to live in my mind, pure and clear.
I want frozen faces
with frozen mouths.

I want to drink too much tonight.
I want to be something else.
I want no name,
and there's no one to blame.

AWAY AND AWAY

They fell for a fantasy
built around assumptions,
and a desire to be reflected
like an infinite mirror.

It was a lot to ask, they know.
They see now,
it was all show and tell.
Mirrors are easily broken -
how could they forget a thing such as this?

They need more than a river now
to cleanse their souls,
to baptize and remove the remnants of
this fallen dream.

They need something more than the moon
to light the darkness they have tumbled into
They need a vein of harsh reality
to recover from the fantastic fall
that took them away and away

GHOST HAS GONE

Where have you been, my ghost -
have you gone the way of the sky?

What have I done, my ghost -
to make you want to forget me now?

I miss you,
      but not your selfish ways
I miss you,
      but not the way you made me feel
I miss you,
      it's been so many days

I had a ghost,
but now that ghost is gone

SUNBURNT SKIES

Two crows fly off the wire
they flap, then caw out twice -
for whom? for what?

Maybe for the hawk
above them
in the sunburnt skies

The hawk soars never flaps -
never shouts in exasperation
instead, it screams freedom

My eyes take on
the view of the hawk,
looking down at cars and
black irritated birds below

There are no lines left to follow now,
no confines to bind -
just an infinity of sunburnt sky
in all directions, and wings to fly

LOOK AT ME

Ego called,
left a message, and wants a callback...
it's due for an appointment in the echo chamber,
wants to be reassured of how valuable, special, and loved it is...
Oh, and it wanted me to make sure I got this last part word for
word:

DON'T FORGET TO LOOK AT ME

Hey, Ego, it's me, calling you back.
You are a bit too vulnerable and needy - a bit too raw and
exposed. Oh, and that echo chamber closed a while ago. Didn't
you know that?

Anyways, we both know the truth -
there is no satisfaction in an echo.
It never lasts long enough.

But, I will look at you if you like, real close up.

OF THE DREAM

There is not enough room for conversation -
only space now for wide monologues that never end.

Are we just to sit silent, rapt at attention,
expected to marvel at every boring thing you say?

This is not talk of the dream.

Perhaps we can bring out our thoughts from our dusty bags and
find each other scattered on the plains after all the others have
ambled off to their makeshift shanty homes

Then we can really talk of the dream.

STONE

Snakes writhe upon your head -
no one seems to appreciate
why you needed a security system
such as this

Powerful eyes
everyone seems to despise
good luck overtaking a woman
such as this

Medusa, I am calling on you now
with one question to ask...
will you turn me into stone
with your vengeful eyes?

I will make an easy job of it for you -
so much of my heart is already cold
so much of my spirit is already hard

I will stay with you forever,
in this garden filled with granite,
under the protection of your eternal primal rage

SIFT THE MEANING LIKE SAND

I never wanted to see this wasteland again, but here I am.
The wide open arms of the Joshua Trees always made me
uncomfortable - so many of them reaching out into the vast dry
hills.

Sift the meaning like sand...

Maybe those open arms aren't so bad - just a bunch of cacti
after all. I'm driving down the old highway, but your house
hasn't been here for a long time.

When you'd pick me up, we would drive into this deep desert,
and you'd drum the beat of a Doobie Brother's tune on the
dashboard. You always knew the best retro diners to stop in.
We'd take our seats at a counter, parallel, not eye to eye, eating
eggs and bacon off melamine plates, no matter what time of
day it was.

You left me to my own devices day after day in the desert heat. I
never minded that part - I was born to be on my own.
I was good at wasting the days away reading old copies of Mad
Magazine, or pretending to be an artist in Paris, putting up my
drawings with tape on the wood-paneled walls of my 'gallery,'
or sitting for hours underneath the only fan to maintain some
normal semblance of body temperature.

All of that was fine - even good at times. It was the woman, her
new name was Joy - I never learned the name she left behind.
She changed her identity to escape a deranged ex-husband who
chased her down their street with a butcher knife. She filled up
most of the space in the double wide with her jealousy and
anger. I learned the word Co-Dependency because she talked
about it so much.

It was clear when she threw away my Mad Magazines and
ripped my 'Paris' gallery off the walls that I was unwanted.
No wonder I've never liked the word Joy.
Hard to be alone with her.

The thunder-lightening opera in the open skies
of Morongo sounded off in the night like gods.
The flashes lit up everything used to being unseen
in the deep desert darkness.

That electric storm raged on the last night I spent being a part
of your life. Joy sat next to me on the covered porch as we
watched the sky show in silence. Did she know it was the last
time I'd be there? I surely didn't.

You left me behind with a brutal final phone call,
and a wound, quick and deep like lightning -
a black hole in my young world. I called to tell you I'd made the
basketball team. You didn't care about that.

I learned later, that the mobile home in Morongo burned down
not long after that phone call, and your dogs died.
Electrical fire - quick, again like lighting, everything lost.
Then you left for the hills of Texas, just like Joy always
dreamed of. When you got there, she left *you* for another man.

I never expected to see you again - you were dead for twenty-
one years, after all. When you came back it was for selfish
reasons. You said you wanted to apologize to me - *owed me at
least that much.* The woman you met after Joy had kids with a
man like you in her youth, and he too left his kids high and dry.
You found him and brought home the deadbeat as a favor.
Maybe you felt that would make up for what you did. But life
doesn't work like that. Your new woman fell in love with her old
man, and when you came to apologize to me it was because you
wanted to kill yourself - which you never did. You aren't good
with promises.

I know the real reason you came back, and it wasn't to say
sorry. I could finally see clearly, as lightning flashed again,
illuminating our darkness. You can keep the money - that's
worthless in comparison to what I got. The meaning of all this
pain sifted like sand. I was released from my prison, free to
leave your living ghost behind, at long last.

WAIT

I willingly give into your plays,
and smooth manipulations
I like the games you make up-
we move in the same dimensions

You come close like a lit flame -
my hand teases over your fire
You pull me in with the promise of warmth,
as you lead me to the pyre

When you have me good and tied,
and things are getting hot,
you drop a thousand ember sparks
heat is pleasant until it's not

BAD LINGUISTICS

Filled to the brim
with too many
things,
people,
places,
ideas -
The nouns of this world
are killing
me

WINDING RIBBON

Say the words I want to hear -
twirl me like a winding ribbon
until I'm dizzy with delight

Come through the back window
like the breeze of late spring,
both warm and cool at the same time

Move around me like the ripples
the lake was made from the stone we threw
How it splashed us made us laugh

Drink me in like the hummingbird sips nectar
from the purple flowers on the porch
Do you think hummingbirds ever get drunk?

When all of these lovely things are done,
come back to the winding ribbon,
and we will begin again

OLD WOMAN

That truck has been through hell -
filled with junk, trash, nonsense
rusted, dented, faded patches of dark green

The driver's side window is tired,
and won't be bothered to get up,
once it's down.

An old woman limps out of the truck
a teenager pops out the other door
In the front of the dented hood,
she checks the girl's scalp for lice
for what seems to be
a very long time.

That old woman isn't so old,
and that old truck isn't much,
but it gets her where she's going -
which is most likely
nowhere.

SHIVER DANCE

She cuts into minds with the sharp end
of her slender sickle,
first bitter, then so sweet -
expanding and letting go
quietly into the dark

Notice how many more stars appear
on nights like these?
No need for speeches
only a dance around the trees,
we are moving for the moon that opened the gate
the moon that released the flood
of some tribal ancient knowing
running in our veins tonight

Feed her reflections of fire in our sweat
so she can take us where we need to go
straight on through an ecstatic vision
of the world as it truly is

FLAME OF THE OLD

I give you too much credit -
think you're attentive like
obsessive like me
compulsive like me,
but you won't even notice a thing,
you're still tangled up
in the flame of the old.

I enter the scene like it's an epic -
an odyssey to be explored -
every little moment,
each detail meant to be etched onto metal plates
recorded in the story pages of antiquity -
while you come in offering
dying embers of the old.

I remember everything you say to me,
but what I say is forgotten fast.
Am I going to survive this journey with you,
or am I destined to drown
in the wet blanket
you keep throwing on my fire?

I can make for you stars out of the dust,
but you only offer in return,
a distant flame of the old.

NOT THE FIRST

You've chosen to leave me now.
That's ok.
Really.
    You're not the first,
    and certainly not the worst one
    I've had to let go of it.

My hands were never
clenched in iron around you.
I hope you know that now.
    I learned long ago to not even try that trick -
    learned early that I couldn't keep hold
    of anyone, or anything in an iron grip.

Things slip away,
everything eventually goes -
both are good and sad, things to know
    I enjoyed your company
    while it lasted.
    Feel free now to go.

THE WORN TIRED GAME

There was a long time
going without

Damn the sirens of addiction
who have her number
who text and call
who leave messages in their seductive songs

Come on, it won't take long
Come on, it won't cost much...

Memories full of forgetting come back,
the desire is hot -
she wants it
The search is on, must find it...
only a small mark on the arm,
it is done...

A never-ending game -
always the same
dryness of the mouth
a cotton feeling on the tongue
gone too far this time
she feels the weight of mountains on her chest

Singers of this sad song,
wail louder than the sirens
of the ambulance
screaming in the distance

DECONSTRUCTION

There is pleasure in this pain
a rusty tear in your eye
you hold out your hand in an offer
to rule the underworld by your side

Don't cry, dear one -
It takes you too far down
into the corridors of Carrion

Let us stay together now
with no words, quiet at last
I am not afraid of this kind of life

I volunteer to be destroyed
smashed to particles
to go beneath the ground
and be fully deconstructed by you

RETURN

I'll love you still
when you
come back home
over those hills.

I know I said I wouldn't,
but that was a lie.

You thought things would be better
out where the lights never dim -

Are they?

Doesn't matter.
Nothing does.

Come back dirty,
come back clean
come back
fixed or broken

Stop more time
from being stolen.
Just come back home to me,
and I'll love you still.

WITH SOMEONE ELSE

I've heard talk of twin flames - always thought it was silly.
There are a lot of flames,
enough to fill a lifetime of different fires
You could be my twin flame, and so could someone else,
any one of many close matches would do fine, and every one of
them would disappoint in some way or another

Thinking there's only one perfect match
just makes people unsatisfied,
as if there's some missing singular puzzle piece
that will fill their insides up -
like a stupid Jerry McGuire, "You complete me,"
type of pleasure to magically last for all time

All time is a long time, forever is forever,
and that's a lot of pressure, isn't it?
So much expectation of fulfillment desire from someone else
when nobody could live up - no such thing as perfect.

Many people feel alone, even when they are part of two
Does coupling forever stop the flow of people growing,
or can you keep resetting with only one partner for a lifetime?

We live so long now - before there was:

death in childbirth
death in war
death in liquid-filled lungs
death in fever
death in a god-dammed sore
that never healed right

Then one day, not too long ago,
excessive youthful death was put on hold
and we became expectant of the longest kind of life

Suddenly repelled by:

struggle love,
sacrifice love
survival mates

Somehow entitled to:

true love
twin flames
soulmates

Fairy tales end at the beginning
of the wedding union for a reason
That's the time for contracts and compromises -
these things are not very romantic, are they?

It all sounds so bleak
but reality usually is in its way
The lights turn on, and that girl
couldn't possibly be the same one
you've been talking to all night at the bar...

To be with one person for a lifetime
is hard no matter what anyone tries to tell you,
but there's a unique beauty in
sharing a victory lap over doing hard things together
and somehow making love last
even when the odds are ever against your favor -
with that one person, or with someone else.

SURRENDER

Here. Take it.
All I have.
Means nothing to me
if it isn't in your hands.
Take all I have.

LIKE VENUS

He makes her feel like Venus -
a queen of love and pleasure
they live in the most beautiful parts
of a world made for two

He makes her into Venus
born from an ocean shell
waiting for him like a pearly dream
an empress to please and be pleased

He looks at her like a Botticelli
full, in all her authenticity
she has nothing to hide -
her curves are rounded, and her flesh is ripe

He sees her as a work of art
with her flaws somehow necessary to the beauty
leaving them free to love
unbounded by restraint

KEEPER

Keep you in my corner
in my back pocket
for when I need something
to bring me back to life
It could be just like heaven
to have a little taste
of you with me all the time
It's a great mystery
how you bring me
back to life

You're a keeper, you are

FINALLY

He finally did something smart
ripped up the envelope
and left it in the trash
alongside a sliver of his heart

He was so close to sticking on a stamp
close to slipping it into the slot
to send all his thoughts to you
in the form of a few pages
ripped from an old library book

He thought, "Where am I going with this?"
The odds were even at the start
but he finally did something smart

IF WE HAD TO LEAVE

It's been so long since I've been tested
I've figured out a way around the hardest exams

There's a price to pay for such luxury,
and there's a hanging on by the fingernails
that happens every day-
a fear that the tower could crumble at any time

What to do then?
I haven't studied -
I haven't practiced,
for a challenge that hard

Yet, how can I ever expect to
reach the next level,
if I never take the tests?

NEVER BEEN GOOD

I'm being cloistered and bricked,
locked into a lifetime of immurement*
sentenced to go *into* peace,
forced *into* goodness -
I've never really been good

How could I have escaped this fate
with the villainous blood I've inherited?
Heresy mixes with the air in my lungs…

I'll be here until I die -
there's no way out now,
the mortar has been set

Perhaps they will still bring me peaches -
then at least I will know
when it is summertime

*In Catholic monastic tradition, there existed a type of enforced, lifelong
confinement against nuns or monks who had broken their vows of chastity
or espoused heretical ideas, and some believed that this type of
imprisonment was, indeed, a form of immurement. The judgment was
preceded by the phrase vade in pacem, that is, "go into peace", rather than
"go in peace".

SOMEONE'S HERO

in one moment,
someone's hero
the next?
far lower than
a sub-basement floor

it's not easy
to traverse
a range
of peaks so high
and valleys so low

just another victim
of circumstance
a fighter
in one's own inner war

DISAPPEAR

I think I'll disappear for a while-
go off the radar
absent without leave

There are so many stars to visit in my mind
and worlds to explore
in the spaces in between

There are portals to places
I could easily disappear
for a very long while indeed

Search with the widest telescope lens
if you must reach me,
and send any messages into space
etched upon a fine gold record

DELUSION

It's a clearer path without you,
but what good is a life with no fantasy?

Devil on my shoulder
Devil in my heart
You're what I thought I wanted
from the start

I have trouble with anything
not part of the fairy dust-coated imagination
pumped up magic feelings
made in the factory of my head

I want to ride the Pegasus again

Is that the start of my mess?
stories of the pegasus mixed with hypnosis,
put me to sleep as a child

From such heights
upon the back of a winged horse,
it all becomes clear
I don't like horses *or* flying.

EXPECTATIONS

I'll never ask, so I'll never know.
That's what makes it beautiful, I suppose -
the not knowing, because it left me glowing,
and reality will never be better than that.

PAISLEY ABBEY

I was the youngest monk of Paisley Abbey
when I pulled the future King
from his mother's jagged womb
She was barely more than a child herself, just like me

She had fallen from her horse,
hit her head with such force,
that she came to us limp, barely alive -
an extinguished spark of flame.

That morning I was sitting still
in worship at the feet of the almighty,
My communion was broken by shocking shouts -
filled with fear that it may already be too late

The cut the Old One made looked unskilled,
quite unsteady from age -
his hands had grown shaky for this kind of delicate work
but this was not something any of us could have said

Salvation for this mother and son
would be no easy task
Yet my hands were young and steady,
and I had a certain skill, despite my age

In the dark room, the floor was slick with blood
the child had been cut through to the eye
with that jagged first slice,
leaving a wound that would never heal right

The birthing didn't take long,
it couldn't of course -
there was a future king to remove
from a collapsing cave

When all was done,
there was no need to tend
the mother's wounds or womb,
because death was built into her child's birth.

Later, alone in my simple room, I tried not to
question why Our Father, or the Old One,
would do such a thing
to any of us.

I left Paisley Abbey soon after,
sent away to harsher lands,
to spend my long lifetime still to come
holding close the hands of death

BLISS

I almost lost my mind
it's not such a bad thing to lose
inhibitions dissolved
restrictions released
not giving a damn about things
I usually care too much about

Oh, simplicity -
how free you are
in your beauty

I almost lost my body
in fits and sparks of glittering pleasure
that rolled like a grassy knoll
of soft reverie...
I could hardly tell
where my body began or ended

Oh, Freedom-
how beautiful you are
in your simplicity

I almost lost my whole self
in a river of twinkling bliss
and it was then,
in that big bang blast,
that I caught a glimpse
of life's elusive truth

Oh, beauty -
how simple you are
in your freedom

ARCHEOLOGY

There are so many layers
stratum of earth
making nothing very simple
when you want to uncover
the truth that lies beneath it all

There are toothbrushes
and paintbrushes to use as tools
ineffective things
for removing eons
of dirt and rocks,
upon more dirt,
upon even more rocks

In the multiverse of levels
we are searching for proof -
for a butterfly trapped in amber
a phosphorescent gram of infinity
a holy grail
existing just inside
but still so hard to reach
beneath these layers

OURANOS

Most ancient,
furthest down the line,
primordial masculine deity of the sky

This is Ouranos maker of the rain
I am his great, great, granddaughter
to the millionth degree

Many others wild and free came before me
and I feel them running in my DNA
We are Ouranos rising set for Revolution

Rebel against the meaningless traps
against stupidity
against over-simplification
and wasters of precious time

Do not forget so quickly
when you are scared by the next sensational story
or frightened by a new star prophecy
being rolled down the conveyor belt all wrong
from our ever-neutral sky

SPACE

There is a deep longing
made by the space
you leave when you leave
I'm calling to you
flashing a beacon
like a lighthouse in the fog
shining for nothing
if you don't return

RELEASE

Locked in a deep abyss
where no light can enter
there are sounds I'll never forget
smells I'll never escape -
the dirty pestilence persists

I'd like to resist the dreary road
that leaves no space for space or stars,
or whatever is behind all of that

I must find someplace quiet
a harbor to anchor my ship
through these emotional king tides

HOW CAN I?

You're so much smarter than I am -
it's one of my favorite things about you
You think I can keep up?
How can I?

I don't understand half of what you say
but I appreciate the vote of confidence.
Still, I don't hold up -
how can I?

You are a pacerunner of the mind
and I am in the back of your pack
heaving and fighting to recapture my breath

I see you in all your brilliance, setting the tempo,
I catch a second wind and think,
"Can I get closer to your speed?"

Keep on being smarter than me -
Perhaps one day
I will figure out how to catch up

TAKEN FOR A RIDE

You drove wild like you were playing an underworld game. Nothing is your fault, babe - we were in it together all the same. Our life was freedom-power fueled by gasoline. Everyone got out of our way back then - maybe 'cause the car had shitty breaks.

A bottomless pitcher of beer, in any dusty honky tonk would classify as home. You always knew what songs I wanted to hear on the jukebox.

We were the best they'd ever seen in any town we rolled up in - remember? Bringing life with our music, our mouths to stale microphones, playing until the last call...

Tell me there's gas in the car - at least enough for one more ride...

Come pick me up again, and we'll travel the endless roads to nowhere - we can let the wheels just spin and spin.

I still have those jeans you loved. Do you still have my hat? More than any of that, do you have it in you to take just one more ride?

UNLOCKED

Magic Man, you are a clever one
with your ring of keys -
each one fitting into some
previously locked and lost place
connecting with unspoken thoughts

The Magic Man knows
his skeleton keys are powerful
but he's kind and will help you see
that you have that power too
But you're not so sure you do...
because you'd give in
if he'd let you,
and be
be totally
undone
by that Magic Man

RESOLUTION 1

It's time to stop dwelling in even one shade of the past hurting heart. It's time to stop using loss as a foundation for identity.

Understand that the act of abandonment has been a form, molding life in complex ways. Hard losses can be a gift even when they hurt worse than hell, and you wouldn't wish the same thing on anyone living and breathing.

It's ok to hurt about what was lost. It's ok to feel sad at the thought of letting go to infinity, over and over of people, places, and things that were cherished. What remains, when you bravely release the hold is strength.

It's time to let go of a desire to control anything - feel free to be a complete mess, and fall in the process — that's the best way to learn.

Think of a baby attempting to walk, and all her failures in the process. Each terrible fall is necessary to reach the goal of standing alone, being independent, and not being stuck in one place. Failure now for freedom later - that's what the baby knows without knowing.

RESOLUTION 2

Once I had thousands of things - books I'd never read, clothes that didn't fit, pictures I hated...then one day, an alarm of awareness sounded, and the time had come to release the physical burden of so many anchors. Goodbye.

Once I sat across from a strange man who inflicted the lion's share of damage to my heart. I looked hard the man I never really knew, a stranger who was designed for a life as my guide. I saw he was holding onto ancient wounds of his own, and they made him incapable of what was meant to be. Goodbye.

Once I was given the priceless gift of emancipation, which allowed an opening of free space in the hard drive of my heart. Old feelings and outdated thoughts? I put them in the bin along with the clothes that didn't fit, and pictures that held memories of pain like a safe deposit box. I learned I could walk pretty well on my own after all those falls.

Once, for a very long time, and even still, I was loved unconditionally by a man who never gave up on me. He saw a potential diamond polished when I just felt like a dull rock. It took a long time, but he had faith, which let me have faith in myself.

Leaving, and being left behind, I realize, were the best things that have ever happened to me, but *being truly loved* is even better.

EPILOGUE

Hey kid -
make me a promise.
tell me you'll be strong

Being strong is only the start
I don't want to hear that you'll '*try*' -
None of that half-assed, half-defeated nonsense
Trying gets you nowhere real
You have to be strong with a relentless drive -
a singular passion to persist -
because when you do this
you get to survive

Surviving is only the start
To get where you need to go
you need to survive all the hard stuff
Even in the moments when you want to give up
promise you won't
because you need to survive
to understand anything at all

Understanding is only the start
Swear you'll push through to understand
even when nothing makes sense,
when you see clear differences and duality everywhere
Especially when you feel like
you don't know anything for sure

Sit with that kid.
You need to understand in order
to *NOT* understand anything
and be at peace with that knowing

Knowing nothing is the first step
towards truly knowing anything worthwhile
Only then are you dipping a baby toe into
the expansive wisdom of all things
Here you can enter a state of awareness

Awareness is only the start
It opens you up to the possibility of surrender
To what you ask?
Surrender to an incomprehensible cosmic consciousness
where there is no such thing as right or wrong, good or bad

Your world doesn't teach things right, kid.
Everything they'll tell you is built on the lie of separation -
the weaker you are, the more you buy that line

Listen, all things are interwoven
Everything is in a state of being intertwined
We are part of something bigger than most minds
can even begin to touch

Be strong so you can survive
Survive so you can understand
Understand so you can be okay with not understanding
that is called wisdom
Be wise to enter a state of awareness
and in that wild place of wide-open eyes
you will be able to surrender
Only through sincere surrender
will you get your first glimpse of infinity…

Then, it's up to you from there, kid.

You can find me at LNatale.com

Printed in Great Britain
by Amazon

39678168R00050